T0158941

THE KEY TO PROBLEM SOLVING

A FOUR STEP SOLUTION

PHYLLIS M. WILSON, PH.D.

authorHOUSE

AuthorHouse™
1663 Liberty Drive
Bloomington, IN 47403
www.authorhouse.com
Phone: 833-262-8899

Published by AuthorHouse 09/11/2020

ISBN: 978-1-7283-7331-7 (sc)
ISBN: 978-1-7283-7330-0 (e)

Library of Congress Control Number: 2020917152

Print information available on the last page.

INTRODUCTION

Everyday of our lives we are faced with issues, problems, obstacles and challenges-some minor and some major. After a series of life lessons based on the many problems that have come my way, I realized that no matter how simple or complex the problem, there were only 4 steps that I applied in each situation. Some of these steps were taken retrospectively as time and distance gave me a whole new view of my experiences.

As we all continue to face life's many challenges, I wanted to arm you with a rich supply of techniques and thought processes you can apply in every situation. Welcome to the new life your new way of thinking will provide.

I was helping my much younger brother find some solutions to a problem he was facing. The problem was the denial of a visa for the Mexican husband he had married a few years back. The visa denial was the result of my brother's decision to purchase a cheaper one- way ticket for himself and his husband after a short stay in the home my brother owned in Colima, Mexico. My brother had no idea that since his husband had not yet been granted the green card visa, his spouse was required to have a round trip ticket

back to Mexico. Little did my brother know that his decision to purchase the one-way, cheaper ticket to Texas and then on to his hometown of Chicago versus a direct flight to Chicago would continue to haunt him when his husband applied for the extended stay visa. My brother's plan to purchase his spouse's return ticket at a later date was viewed as a violation of immigration rules and regulations. Rules and regulations he had no idea existed.

When my brother called me from Mexico crying and in distress because his spouse was prohibited from accompanying him back to Chicago, I immediately began thinking about who I knew and how each person I knew could help. It was during this time frame when I was

assisting my brother with his very serious problem that I had an epiphany. My epiphany was that all of my life I had handled any problem, any obstacle, any challenge, any issue in the same manner. My manner was to apply four very specific and basic set of steps. Steps which led to the actions that followed. It took me many years to come to this realization. I want to provide a short cut for you-a way to decisive and impactful actions. Let us begin.

STEP ONE

The first step in the problem resolution process is the appearance of whatever is causing you stress and concern. Once this concern appears, the person affected must answer the following questions:

What is the problem/concern?

What did I do to cause this concern?

How do I respond to the challenge or concern?

Am I calm? Upset? Angry? Dumbfounded? Stupefied?

These questions must be asked because it is the emotion that is first felt that will impact every action taken beyond this point. The reason is because for every response or feeling, an action will follow. Without careful thought the action or response could well be the wrong one.

If you are calm, you will begin to think logically and rationally about the next steps that will be taken. If you are upset or angry, your next steps might involve actions that seek revenge or hurt for the person who has perpetrated the action upon you. If you are stupefied or dumbfounded, you may enter the fog of inaction and victimization that leaves you stuck in one place. This first step

is the most critical one of all the steps because you will either be motivated to move forward; or, you will be forever standing in the bubble or shield you place around yourself. The choice you make will significantly impact your life choices and the person you will become.

STEP TWO

For those who choose to move forward and take action, the next question will be "What can I do?" This is the best method for determining all of the options available to you whether it is through a written list that you develop or a mental list that you run through. This is a critical time because as you sort through the list of available options, it is essential that you select those options that will obtain the best possible results. Questions

that you may need to apply to your list of options include:

Which option will work best?

What is my desired results or outcome?

Which of the available options will achieve the results/outcomes I am seeking?

Am I missing anything in the options list?

Are there other options?

Are these the best and only options?

What will I need to put the options I choose in place?

Who are the other people I need to involve?

Once you have answered all of the questions, you can now decide what you will do; and, prepare for the next step. In my brother's situation, I identified two possible resources who could be of the most assistance for this particular situation. The first resource was a person I knew in an elected official's office in my brother's state. The second resource was the daughter of a friend. The daughter was responsible for issuing visas in another country. I reached out to both of these resources and connected them directly with my brother so that they could provide the much needed assistance, advice, and guidance. Now, we were moving forward to the next step.

STEP THREE

Now that you have completed the exploration of available options, it is time for you to use all of the information you have gathered. Having thoroughly reviewed the options that best fit your circumstances, you can now spend the time you need to develop an action plan. Your action plan should include specific goals for what you hope to accomplish; and, the final outcome you hope to achieve. This will help to ensure that the results that are desired and so important to you are most

likely to occur. What you decide to do at this phase of the decision making process will shape your response to the challenges of life forever after. Questions that you need to ask during this phase are:

Do I need a long term or short term result?

Who can best help me implement the actions I need to take?

How quickly can the plan be implemented?

What do I expect the outcome to be?

Is this the outcome I want?

What is the best way to keep track of the many irons I have in the fire?

Once these questions have been answered, it is time to move to the next and final step.

STEP FOUR

This is the time of action on your part. The questions that will rise to mind are:

What will I do?

What steps will be taken?

Who will be involved and included in the actions I take?

Who will be excluded?

What measures must I take to guarantee success?

What else needs to be done?

Step Four is also the phase when you stop; take a deep breath; and, carefully review all that has been done to solve the problem you face. These actions will precipitate your final most critical questions of all:

Have I achieved the desired and expected outcome?

If not, how close am I to achieving my desired outcome?

If your outcome has been achieved then you

can exhale, do a happy dance and move on, knowing that you are well prepared for the next life challenge that comes your way. And, for sure, there will be many more.

A RETROSPECTIVE LOOK

One of the self revelations that occurred for me as I maneuvered my brother through this very critical time, was that whenever I had been faced with life's many challenges and obstacles, I had often moved quickly through the problem resolution process depending on the issue I was dealing with. Many times I went quickly through the process I have shared with you, going from Step One straight to Step Four. I am a doer, a get things done quickly, take action, take no

prisoners kind of person. These characteristics had contributed to my highly successful career. They had also helped me rise from the ashes of life I sometimes experienced. I realized, however, that not carefully matriculating through the four steps I have described also created times when I had to return back to Step One and begin again for the careful decisions my life choices required.

There were a series of questions that I applied to my retrospective considerations after each problem was solved. They are as follows:

What was the problem?

What did I do? (Actual actions)

What could I have done? (All other options available at the time)

What should I have done? (A review of actions that would have led to a different outcome)

And, now what? (How will I move forward using all that I have gained for the situation I faced).

It is my hope that all that has been shared with you will make you well prepared to move forward in your life knowing that you have all that you need to solve anything that comes your way. You are a winner who can beat the odds. Good luck.

P:S: My brother reached out to both of the resources I recommended; and, an attorney who specializes in immigration matters. Utilizing the feedback and assistance he received from everyone, he completed an appeal on his spouse's behalf. He is currently waiting for a decision (The coronavirus pandemic may now delay the appeal review timelines). My brother feels very optimistic about the outcome of his appeal.